POKÉMON
Gotta catch 'em all!™

HOW TO DRAW

KALOS EDITION

P9-CQH-173

WRITTEN BY MARIA S. BARBO
ILLUSTRATED BY RON ZALME

ISBN 978-0-545-69890-0

10 9 8 7 6   16 17 18 19/0

Designed by Cheung Tai
Printed in the U.S.A.   40
First printing, September 2014

SCHOLASTIC INC.

DRAW 'EM ALL!

Are you ready to become a Pokémon drawing champ? Get in gear! You will need:

- **Pencil** — Any basic graphite pencil should do the trick.
- **Paper** — Photocopy paper or tracing paper is terrific for sketching.
- **Eraser** — Try a soft one that won't smudge and has edges to get into tight spots.
- **Rulers, circle guides, ellipse (oval) guides, and shaped curves** — These help create a smooth, finished look for your drawing.
- **Color** — Try pens, markers, colored pencils, watercolors, paints, etc.

You may also want:

- A thin black marker
- Colored pencils
- Crayons
- Markers
- Watercolors and brushes
- Scrap paper

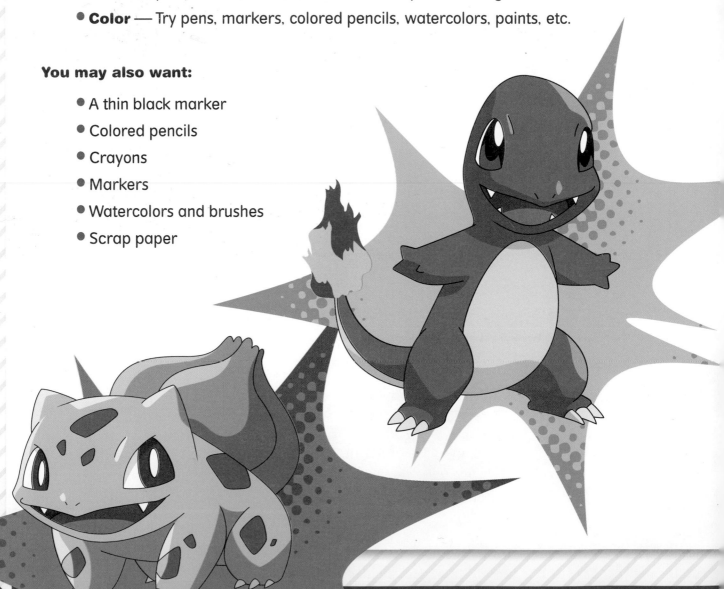

Getting Started:
WARM UP!

Step 1: Get loose! Shake out your arms.

Step 2: Stay loose! Practice drawing circles, squares, triangles, jellybeans, teardrops, squiggles, curvy lines, wavy lines, straight lines, and zigzags.

Step 3: Don't stress! Learning to draw takes time, practice, and lots of patience.

Top Five Training Tips

1. **Back to basics.** Start each drawing with the biggest, most basic steps. Save the details for the end.

2. **Lighten up.** Keep your lines light at first. They'll be easier to erase or draw over.

3. **Break it down.** Practice the hardest parts of each drawing on scrap paper before adding them to your masterpiece.

4. **Work smudge-free.** Keep a piece of scrap paper under your drawing hand so you don't smudge your picture.

5. **Dark over light.** Color in the lightest parts of each Pokémon first. If you use markers or paint, wait until the light colors are 100% dry before you add the dark parts. That way, your colors won't run into each other.

Spheres, cones, cubes, cylinders, and pyramids are the three-dimensional shapes that an artist must *think* in while drawing! Thinking in 3-D helps create the illusion of depth and volume in your artwork. It makes your final drawing look more convincing.

SWIRLIX
Cotton Candy Pokémon

Swirlix's love of sweet snacks makes its fur as sticky as cotton candy. Here's a tip: To keep your hands from sticking to your drawing, keep a piece of scrap paper between you and the paper.

2

Add the basic shapes of the face, legs, tail, and the puffs on top of Swirlix's head. Use your guidelines to help you. Now stop and take a look. Are all the features where you want them to be?

1

Start by drawing a big circle. Then draw one vertical guideline and two curved horizontal guidelines. The top line shows where the eyes and nose will go. The bottom line is for the mouth.

3

Ready to focus on details? Add a small oval inside each eye and a tongue sticking out of the mouth. Draw curves around the outline of Swirlix's body to make it look puffy, like a cotton ball. Then draw a tail at the bottom.

4

Erase extra lines and smudges. When you color Swirlix, try using the white of the paper for the body and light lavender for the shadows. Does your Swirlix look like it's ready to spring off the page?

GOOMY
Soft Tissue Pokémon

This Dragon-type Pokémon is covered with a slippery membrane that makes its opponent's punches and kicks slide right off it. Goomy protects this membrane from the sun by taking shelter in damp, dark places. Remember to keep your drawing of Goomy away from the sun, too! Bright colors fade in direct sunlight.

2

Draw two small dark ovals for eyes, one on each side of the vertical guideline. Then add two long upside-down U-shapes to the top of Goomy's head. Next, replace the bottom line of its body with a wavy line.

1

Start by drawing a big circle. Then attach a few curved lines that look like a cape. Keep your lines light at first— that way, they'll be easy to erase or draw over.

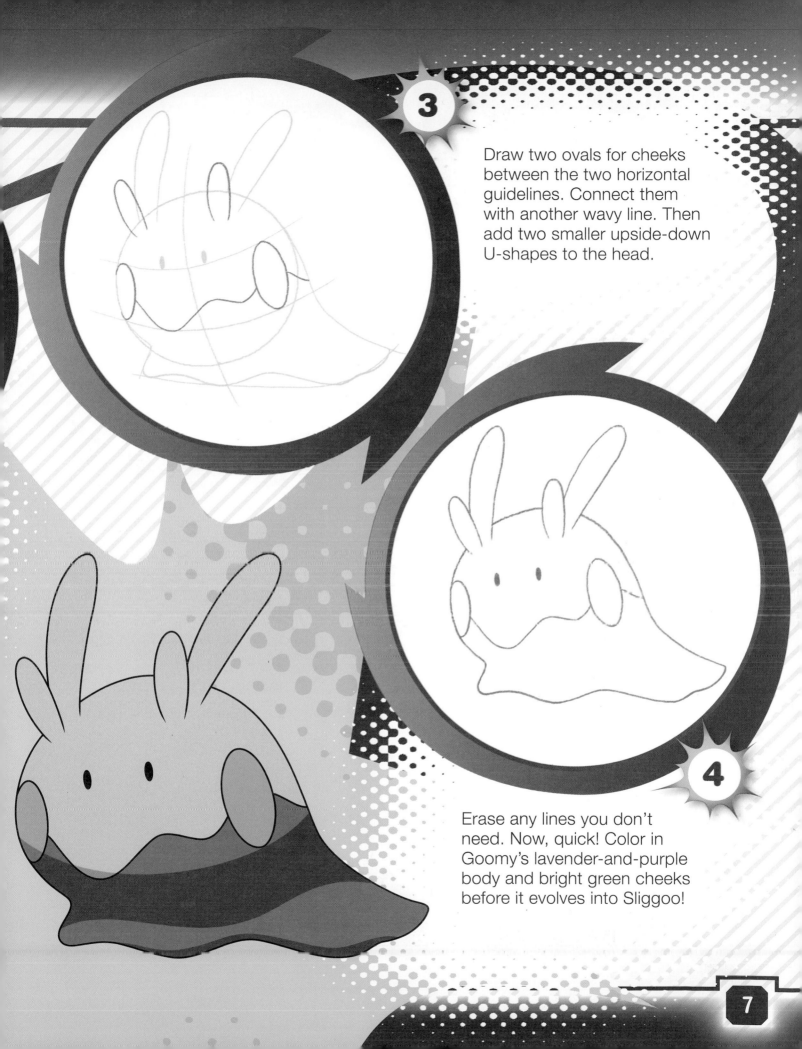

3

Draw two ovals for cheeks between the two horizontal guidelines. Connect them with another wavy line. Then add two smaller upside-down U-shapes to the head.

4

Erase any lines you don't need. Now, quick! Color in Goomy's lavender-and-purple body and bright green cheeks before it evolves into Sliggoo!

DEDENNE
Antenna Pokémon

Dedenne's whiskers are a very important part of this drawing. Dedenne uses them like antennae to send long-distance messages via electrical waves. It also uses them to store up electrical energy for powerful moves like Thunder Wave and Volt Switch.

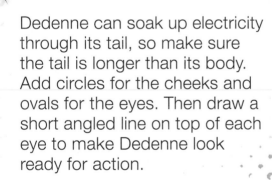

2

Dedenne can soak up electricity through its tail, so make sure the tail is longer than its body. Add circles for the cheeks and ovals for the eyes. Then draw a short angled line on top of each eye to make Dedenne look ready for action.

1

Start with two curved guidelines. Then draw the basic shapes for Dedenne's body. The ovals for the head and body should overlap.

3

Now that the basic outline of the body is in place, it's time to add details. Draw the antennae-like whiskers. Then add fingers, toes, a tongue, and a star shape at the tip of the tail.

4

Almost done! Erase the starter shapes. Then break out the colors! Color in the lightest parts of Dedenne's body first. If you use markers or paint, wait until the lightest brown is 100% dry before you paint the darker browns and red on top. That way, your colors won't run into each other!

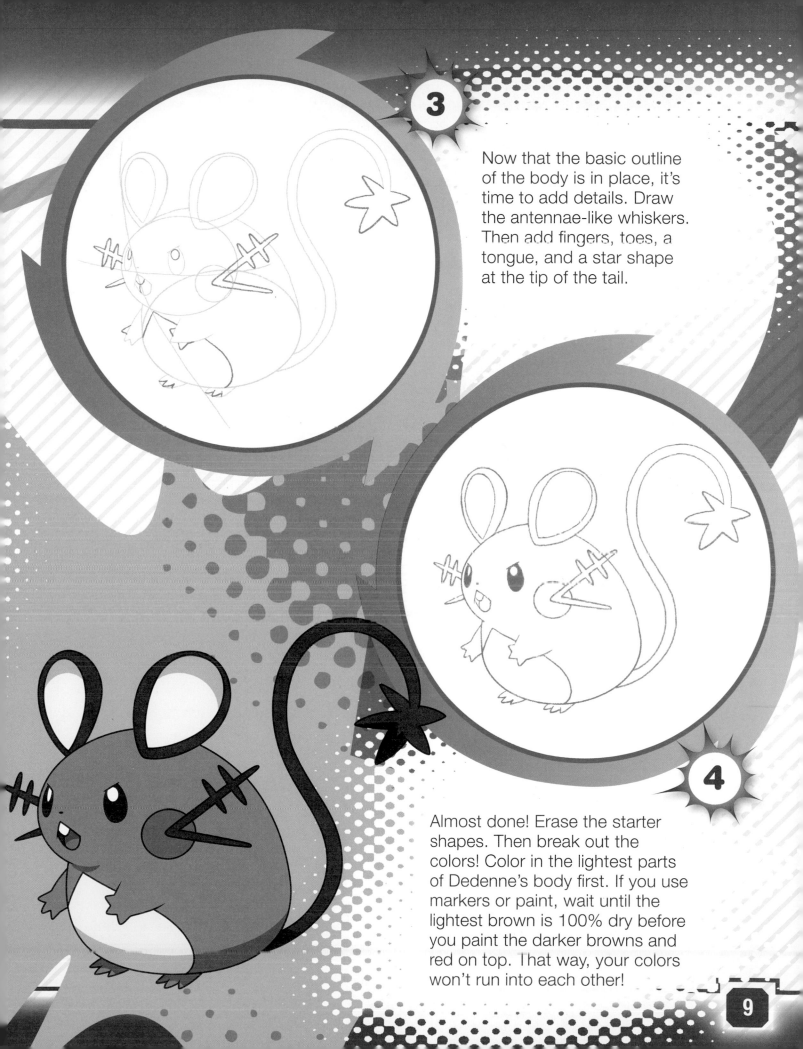

CHARMANDER
Lizard Pokémon

Get out your reds, oranges, and yellows! The glowing flame on the tip of this Fire-type's tail shows that Charmander is in great shape. Are you in great shape for drawing? Warm up by scribbling basic shapes and lines on scrap paper.

2

Take a good look at Charmander's face. The eyes are set as wide as this Fire-type's smile. Now draw the outline of a flame on the tip of Charmander's tail.

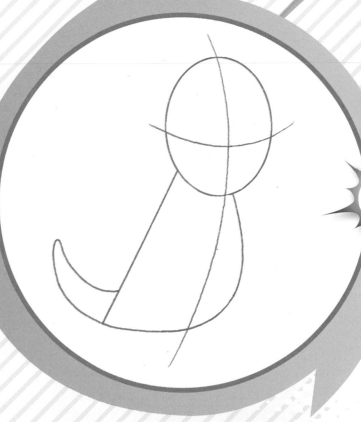

1

Use this step to set up the entire drawing. How big is the head compared to the body? Where does the tail connect to the body? Don't worry about how your drawing looks at this stage. Just get down the basics.

3

Take a minute to reshape the outline of Charmander's body. If you get confused, look at the final drawing to guide you. Then add details like teeth, eyes, claws, and more flames. Don't forget to add the curve of Charmander's belly!

4

Erase extra lines and smudges. Now stand back and compare your drawing to the one in the book. Is anything missing? Does one leg look like it's in front of the body while the other is behind it? If not, make sure you erased the right lines.

BULBASAUR
Seed Pokémon

Bulbasaur uses the big seed bulb on its back to soak up nutrients from the sun. This Grass-and Poison-type has powerful Moves like Razor Leaf and Vine Whip. Are you ready to show off your mighty drawing moves? Then let's take on Bulbasaur!

2

Draw a squished-heart shape for the mouth. Then add loose triangles for the eyes. Now sketch in the seed on Bulbasaur's back and three chubby legs. The lines for the legs closest to you go up and over the body. The lines for the legs farthest away from you are hidden behind the body.

1

Start by breaking this drawing down into the simplest shapes. For Bulbasaur, that's a big, boxy head and half an oval for the body.

3

Add details like spots on the skin and tiny triangles for the teeth and toenails. Inside each eye, draw a curved line next to an oval. Then add curves to the bulb on Bulbasaur's back.

4

Erase the guidelines you drew in Step One, and make any final corrections. Now that you know how to draw Bulbasaur, try drawing it in action. Add vines popping out of the seed on its back for Vine Whip!

SQUIRTLE
Tiny Turtle Pokémon

Squirtle hides inside its shell for protection, but fights back with winning Water-type Moves like Aqua Tail and Water Gun. Once you learn how to draw Squirtle, you can use your winning moves to take on its more evolved forms: Wartortle, Blastoise, and Mega Blastoise.

2

Squirtle's right leg sticks straight out, but the left leg is bent. Position the arms at an angle next to Squirtle's head. If you squint your eyes, the whole body should look like the letter X.

1

The guidelines in this drawing are slanted. That's because Squirtle is leaning to the side, ready for action. Use the angled guidelines to sketch in the basic shapes of Squirtle's body and a curlicue for the tail.

3

Detail time! Finish off the tail and shell with curved lines. Then draw two curved lines inside the mouth for the tongue and use zigzags for the fingers and toes. Study the different shapes inside the eyes before you draw them. For the pattern on Squirtle's tummy, start with a star, and then erase the pointy tips.

4

Almost done! Erase any lines that are getting in the way. Does Squirtle look like it's ready to unleash a Rain Dance? Try drawing a burst of water blasting out of Squirtle's mouth, or some match-winning bubbles!

CHESPIN
Spiny Nut Pokémon

Look out, opponents! When Chespin flexes its soft quills, they become tough spikes with sharp, piercing points. It relies on its nutlike shell for protection in battle, so use a bright green to make it pop!

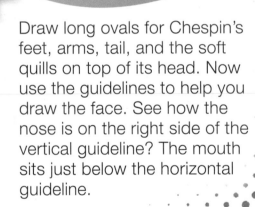

2

Draw long ovals for Chespin's feet, arms, tail, and the soft quills on top of its head. Now use the guidelines to help you draw the face. See how the nose is on the right side of the vertical guideline? The mouth sits just below the horizontal guideline.

1

Start by drawing two crisscrossed guidelines. The spot where they meet will be the center of the face. Draw a circle inside a circle to start. Then draw the basic shapes of the body and quills.

3

Remember all those curves you practiced in the warm-up? Use them now to start adding details like Chespin's tongue, tooth, and toes. Then stand back and take a good look at your drawing. Are any details missing?

4

Time for the fun part! Erase any lines you don't need. Then add color. Chespin's quills are a bright grass green, and the tip of its tail is a dazzling red. When the color is done, you can trace over the outlines with a thin black marker.

LITLEO
Lion Cub Pokémon

When a young Litleo is ready to grow stronger, it spends time on its own developing moves like Flamethrower and Noble Roar. Don't worry about making mistakes as your drawing grows stronger. Learning to draw Pokémon takes time and lots of practice.

2

Draw more circles for the back paw, tail, eyes, and ears. Then connect the front paws to the body with straight lines. Use the guidelines to help you position the nose and mouth between the eyes. Is your drawing already starting to look like Litleo?

1

Start your drawing of Litleo with lots of circles. What's the secret to drawing round circles? Sometimes, the faster you draw them, the rounder they turn out. Go ahead and practice on scrap paper first.

3

This step is all about details. Pick a starting point like the paw pads and make sure you draw them all. Connect the back leg to the body with two short curved lines. Don't forget the tuft of hair on top of Litleo's head.

4

Erase extra lines and get ready to color! During a battle, Litleo's mane gives off intense heat. That's why it's red while the rest of the body is shades of brown!

FROAKIE
Bubble Frog Pokémon

In this pose, Froakie is super-alert to any changes in its environment. The foamy white bubbles that cover its turquoise body protect this Water-type Pokémon's sensitive skin from damage. When you're ready to color in Froakie's bubbles, try letting the white of the paper show through.

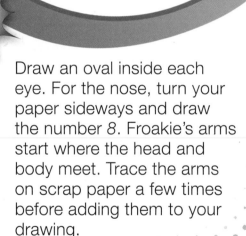

2

Draw an oval inside each eye. For the nose, turn your paper sideways and draw the number *8*. Froakie's arms start where the head and body meet. Trace the arms on scrap paper a few times before adding them to your drawing.

1

Start by drawing the shape of a football. Then add two upside-down *U*s on top for the eyes. Finish up with a rectangular body. Now stop and do a quick check. Are all the shapes where you want them to be?

3

Inside the left edge of each eye, draw an oval inside an oval. Does Froakie look watchful? Now, take your time and draw the back legs. Using half-circles and curves, draw the foamy bubbles that protect Froakie's sensitive skin.

4

Stand back and check your drawing. Which lines need to be erased? Which lines need to be darker? Does Froakie have three fingers on its hands, but only two on its back legs? Did you remember to add the dark blue stripe between the eyes? Great! Now finish off your drawing with color!

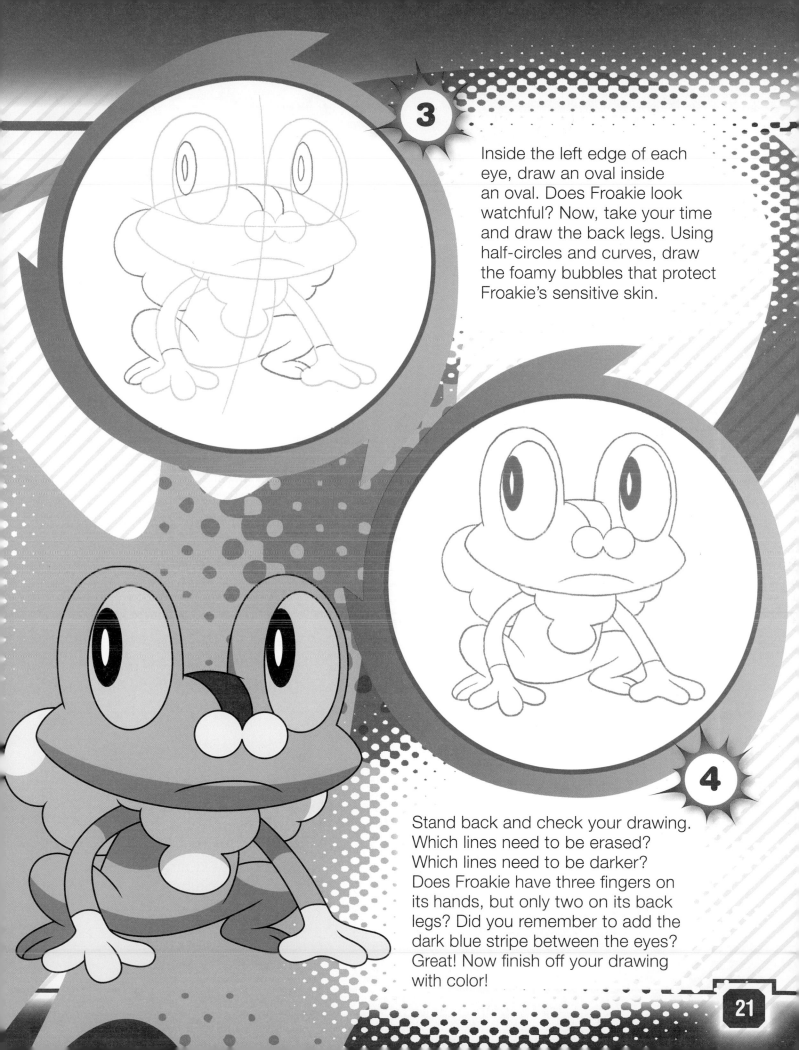

BUNNELBY
Digging Pokémon

Bunnelby's ears are as long as its entire body! Bunnelby uses them like shovels to dig big holes in the ground and for moves like Double Slap and Mud-Slap. The ears are so strong, they can even dig through thick tree roots!

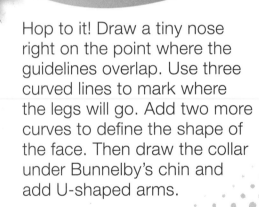

2

Hop to it! Draw a tiny nose right on the point where the guidelines overlap. Use three curved lines to mark where the legs will go. Add two more curves to define the shape of the face. Then draw the collar under Bunnelby's chin and add U-shaped arms.

1

Use this step to set up your drawing. Draw the guidelines closer to the left side of the body for a three-quarter view. What shape is the head? Which way will Bunnelby face? How big are the ears compared to the body?

3

There are lots of details in this step, so take your time. Draw whiskers, spots, and two front teeth. Don't forget the tail, fingers, and teardrop shapes inside the ears.

4

Call in the cleanup crew! Erase any extra lines, smudges, or mistakes. Then color in this Normal-type Pokémon with shades of brown and gray before it bounces off the page!

FENNEKIN
Fox Pokémon

The warm, orangy-red details in this Fire-type's ears, eyes, and tail warn opponents that Fennekin means business. Fennekin likes to charge up before a match by snacking on twigs. You might want to grab a healthy snack to get energized for drawing!

2

Fennekin's pointy nose sits on the horizontal guideline. Draw an oval for the eye where the two guidelines meet. Then sketch in some curved lines where you want to draw the second ear. Next, add a fat teardrop for the tail. Practice the legs on scrap paper before adding them to your drawing.

1

Lightly sketch in guidelines. Use them to figure out where to draw the oval for Fennekin's head and the jellybean shape for its body. Then add a curvy triangle for the ear.

3

Take your time drawing the details on Fennekin's body. Those ears and tail are important! Fennekin uses its plush tail for blazing moves like Tail Whip and Fire Spin, and its ears blast intense heat to keep opponents far away.

4

Erase the lines you don't need. Now step back and take a good look at your drawing. Are the ears as big as the body? How about the legs? Make any tiny fixes, and you're ready to color!

PANCHAM
Playful Pokémon

For a small Pokémon, Pancham has big moves like Body Slam, Crunch, and Karate Chop. You have big decisions to make before you start to draw. Will your drawing of Pancham take up the whole paper? Or will it leap off the page?

2

Use the guidelines to help you position the shapes in the face. Then connect the head to the body with a big, upside-down *U*. Next, draw the arms on an angle. The right arm looks shorter than the left because it's farther away.

1

Decide where to place Pancham on the paper. Then lightly sketch in guidelines and some basic shapes. The vertical guideline is slanted to give a sense of motion.

3

Clean up the outline of Pancham's body. Then start at the top and add details like a zigzag of hair, ovals inside the eyes, and another zigzag for the teeth. Don't forget to draw a leafy sprig next to the mouth. This leaf helps Pancham track its opponents' movements.

4

Do you need to make any changes to your drawing? Does Pancham look like it's leaping into the air? If not, maybe its bottom paws are not high enough. When you're ready, get out your colors. Here's a tip: Use a darker color for the inside of the mouth than for the tongue.

SYLVEON
Intertwining Pokémon

Sylveon is an evolved form of Eevee, and drawing it can be a challenge. You may want to practice drawing big sweeping S curves before you draw the ribbon-like feelers Sylveon uses to calm down its opponents.

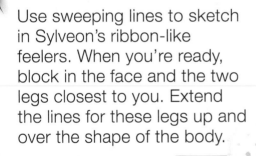

2

Use sweeping lines to sketch in Sylveon's ribbon-like feelers. When you're ready, block in the face and the two legs closest to you. Extend the lines for these legs up and over the shape of the body.

1

Start with guidelines and basic shapes to get an overall sense of Sylveon's body. Then draw a third guideline where you think the ground should be. This line will help you draw the legs in the next step. If you angle the guideline slightly, the back legs will be a tiny bit shorter than the front legs. This is a great trick for making them look farther away.

3

Now draw the two legs farthest from you. Did you notice that some of the lines are hidden behind the body and other legs? Now add details to the face, paws, and ribbons. Don't forget the bows!

4

Compare your drawing to the one in the book. Do you need to make any changes? Now's the time! Are the legs the right size and shape? Are any details missing? Did you keep the line that separates Sylveon's back right leg from the body? Good job! When you're ready, color this Fairy-type Pokémon in shades of pale pink and blue.

TYRUNT
Royal Heir Pokémon

This Rock- and Dragon-type Pokémon has powerful jaws that could crush a car! It also has mighty moves like Earthquake, Dragon Claw, and Stomp. Tyrunt lived millions of years ago, but your drawing will be brand-new. Practice the hard parts on scrap paper before you start.

2

The oval you drew in Step One shows where Tyrunt's massive leg connects to its body. Draw a small arm right in front of the oval. Then add a tail and a zigzag around its neck. Now, focus on the jaw. It juts out from the circle you drew for the head.

1

Step one is all about the big decisions. Will your drawing of Tyrunt take up the whole page or just a small part? Draw the guidelines closer together this time. Then sketch in the basic shapes. Tyrunt is leaning forward, so the head and body fall on the same horizontal line.

3

Draw in the back leg. Then take some time to add details. If they look confusing, pick a place to begin, such as the tail. Then add other details bit by bit—like the half rectangles on the back leg, the fang, and the horns on its head.

4

Erase extra lines and smudges. Now, double-check your drawing. Does anything need fixing up? Is the head almost the same size as the body? Did you draw claws on the hands and feet? Good job! You did it!

Congratulations!
You're a Pokémon Drawing Champion!

Now that you know how to draw so many powerful Pokémon from the Kalos region, what kinds of adventures will you draw? What stories will you tell?

Froakie evolving into Frogadier?
Pancham challenging Tyrunt with a mighty Comet Punch?
Or Sylveon hugging its Trainer with its soothing ribbonlike feelers?

Use your imagination—what happens next is up to you!